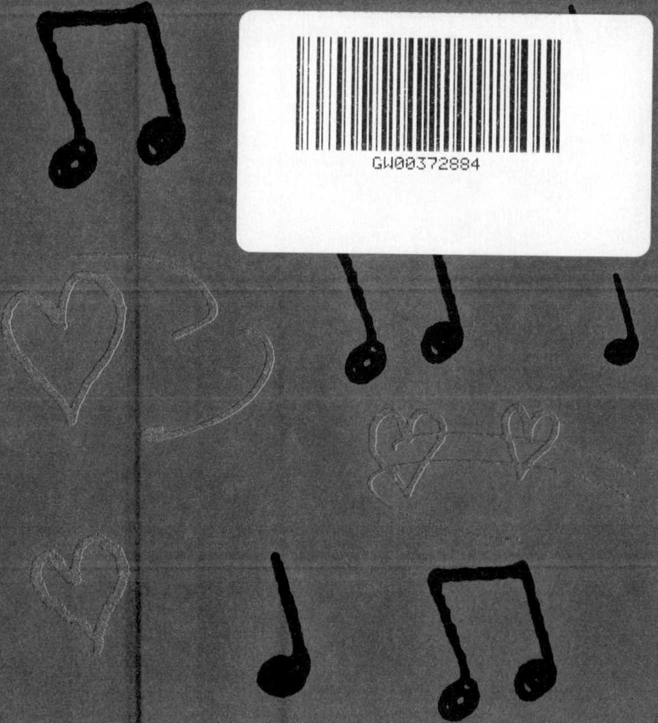

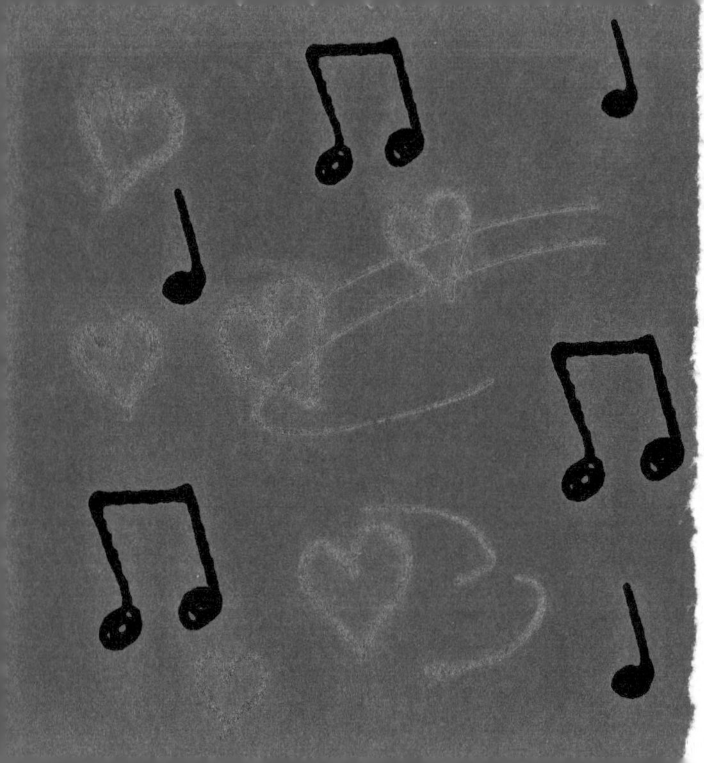

# Love Is In The Air

*by*
*SCHULZ*

BOXTREE

# Love Notes

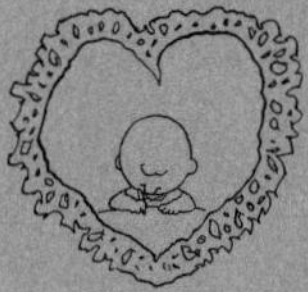

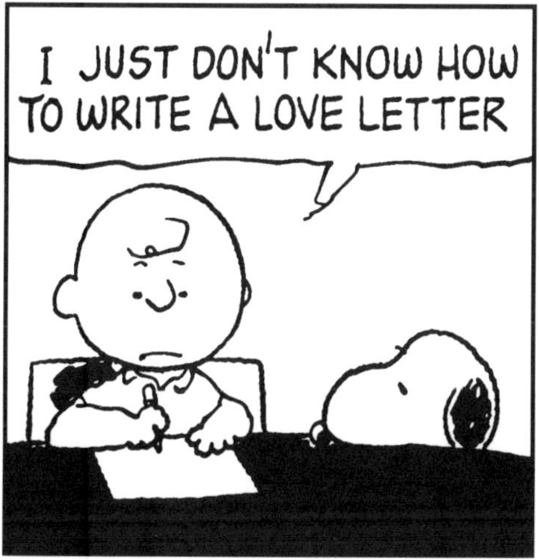
I JUST DON'T KNOW HOW TO WRITE A LOVE LETTER

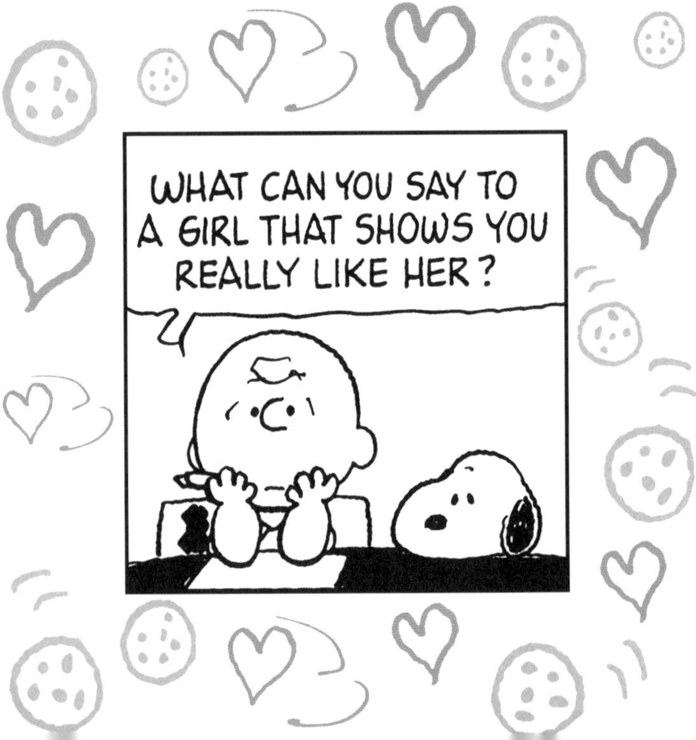
WHAT CAN YOU SAY TO A GIRL THAT SHOWS YOU REALLY LIKE HER?

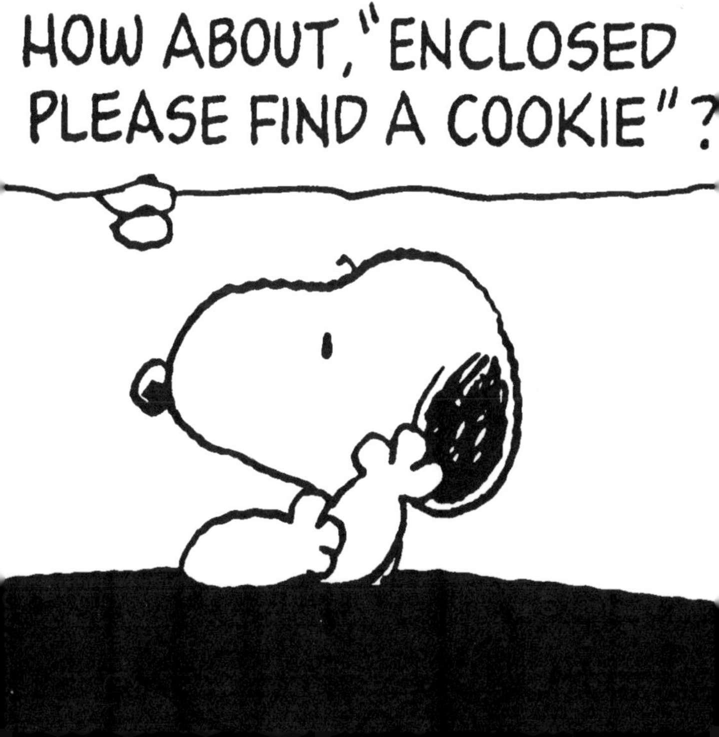
HOW ABOUT, "ENCLOSED PLEASE FIND A COOKIE"?

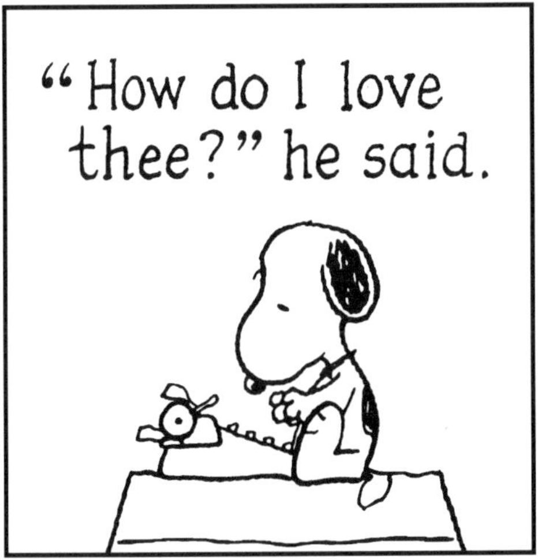
"How do I love thee?" he said.

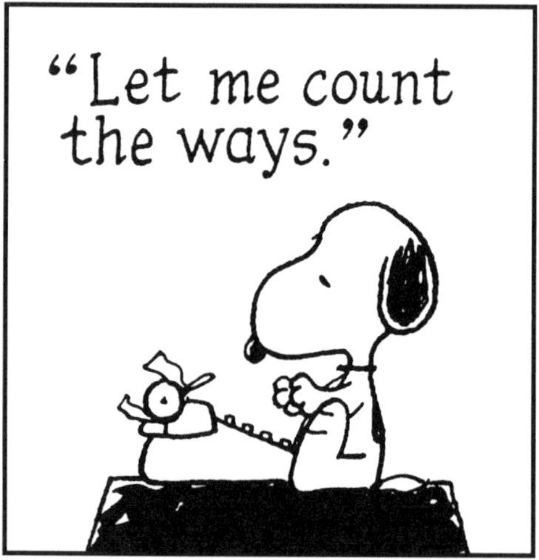
"Let me count the ways."

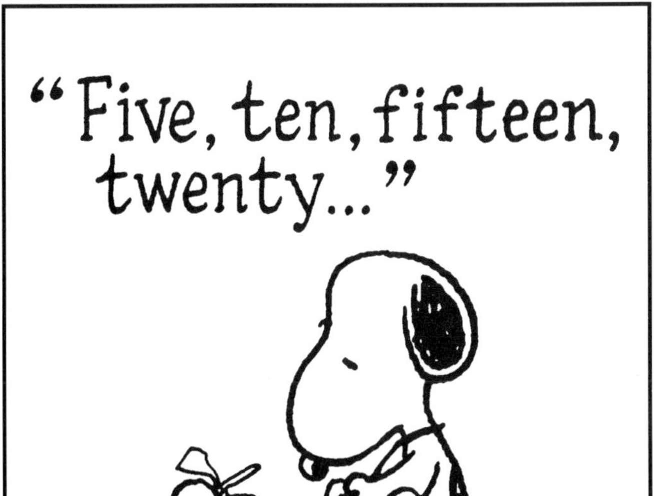
"Five, ten, fifteen, twenty..."

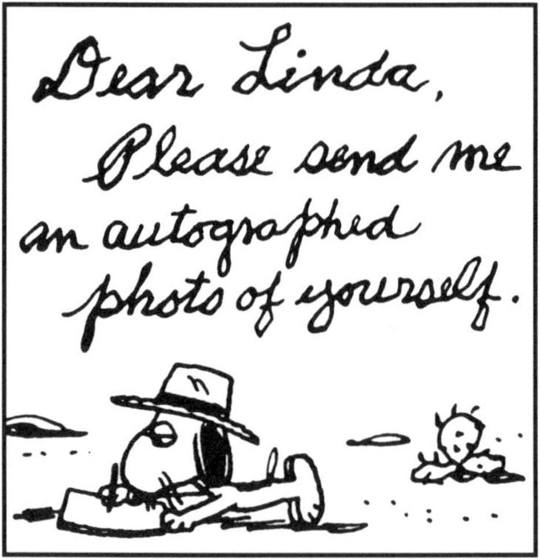

Dear Linda,
Please send me
an autographed
photo of yourself.

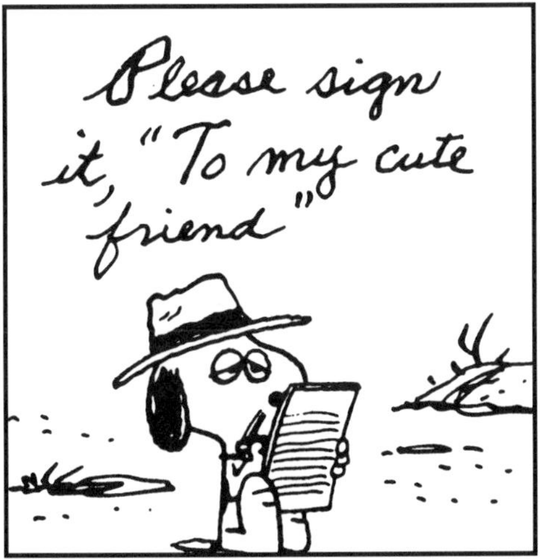
Please sign it, "To my cute friend"

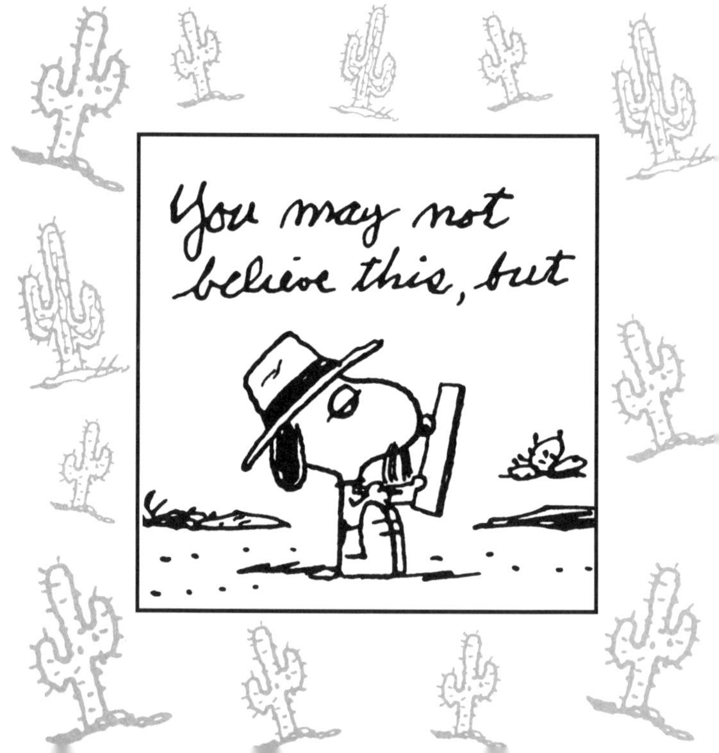
You may not believe this, but

I'm the cutest thing around here.

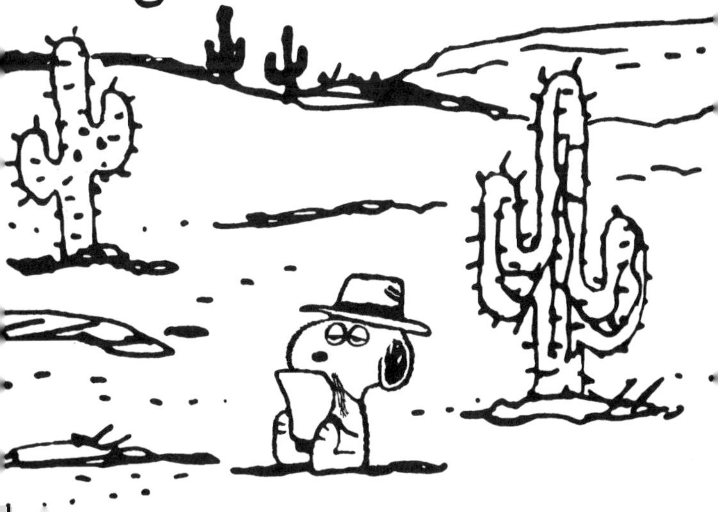

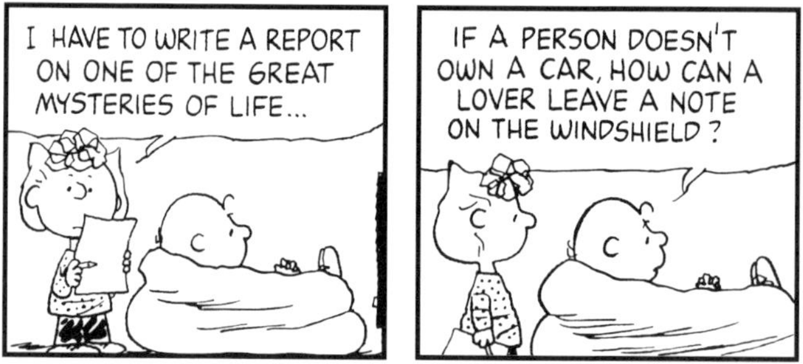
I HAVE TO WRITE A REPORT ON ONE OF THE GREAT MYSTERIES OF LIFE...
IF A PERSON DOESN'T OWN A CAR, HOW CAN A LOVER LEAVE A NOTE ON THE WINDSHIELD?

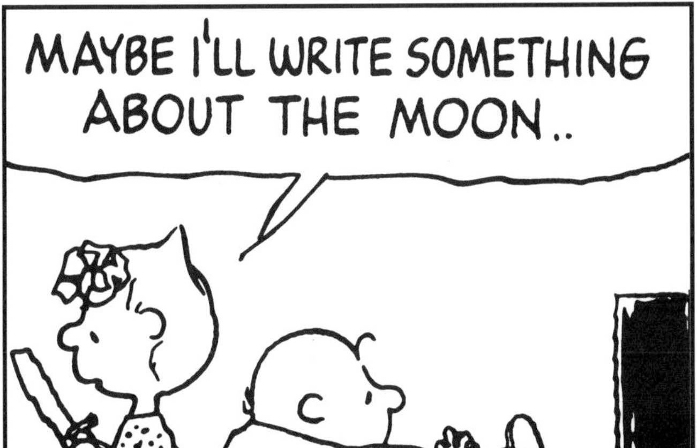
MAYBE I'LL WRITE SOMETHING ABOUT THE MOON..

# It Must Be Love

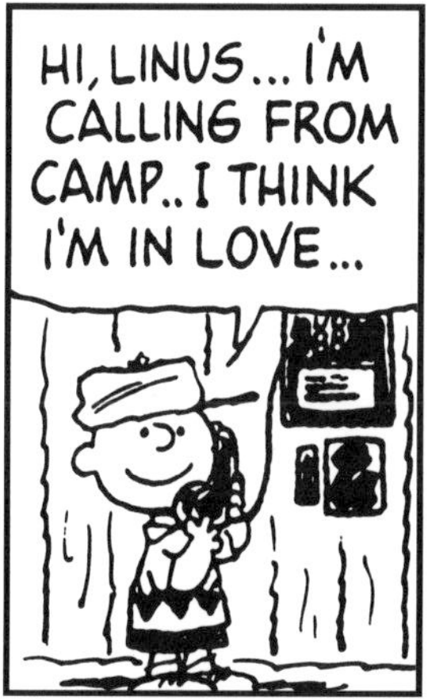
HI, LINUS... I'M CALLING FROM CAMP.. I THINK I'M IN LOVE...

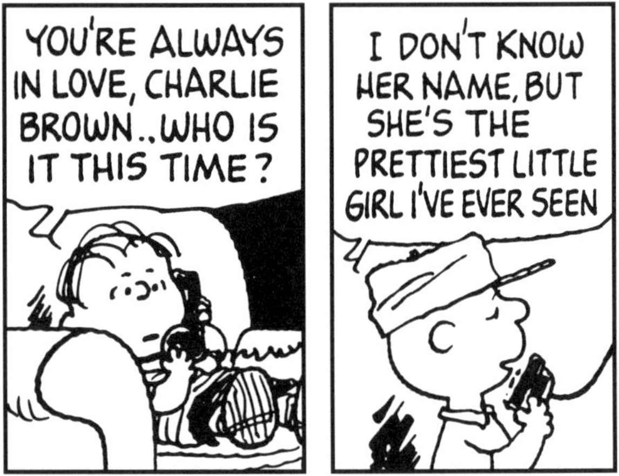
YOU'RE ALWAYS IN LOVE, CHARLIE BROWN.. WHO IS IT THIS TIME?
I DON'T KNOW HER NAME, BUT SHE'S THE PRETTIEST LITTLE GIRL I'VE EVER SEEN

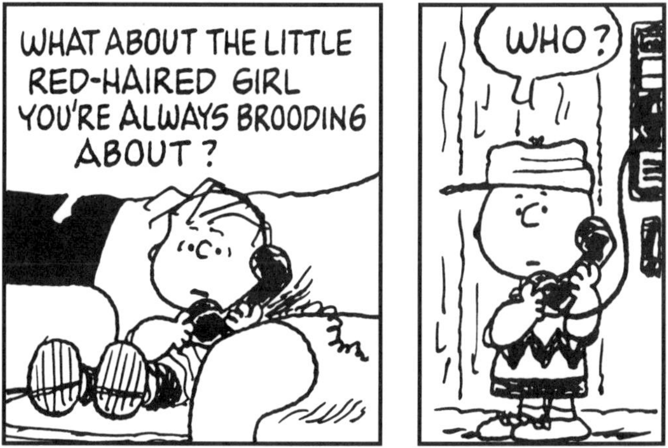
WHAT ABOUT THE LITTLE RED-HAIRED GIRL YOU'RE ALWAYS BROODING ABOUT?
WHO?

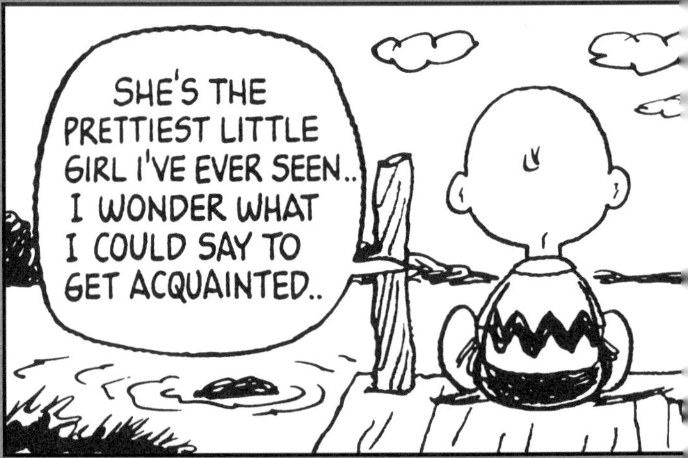
SHE'S THE PRETTIEST LITTLE GIRL I'VE EVER SEEN.. I WONDER WHAT I COULD SAY TO GET ACQUAINTED..

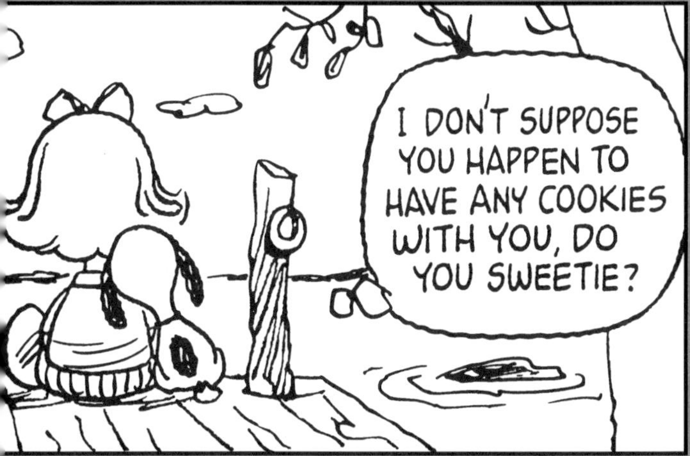
I DON'T SUPPOSE YOU HAPPEN TO HAVE ANY COOKIES WITH YOU, DO YOU SWEETIE?

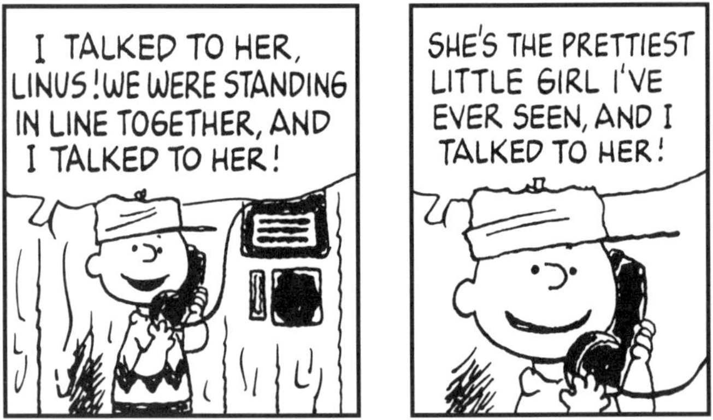
I TALKED TO HER, LINUS! WE WERE STANDING IN LINE TOGETHER, AND I TALKED TO HER!
SHE'S THE PRETTIEST LITTLE GIRL I'VE EVER SEEN, AND I TALKED TO HER!

OH, I GUESS I DIDN'T TELL YOU.. THIS IS ME, LINUS... I'M CALLING AGAIN FROM CAMP...
I KIND OF FIGURED IT WAS YOU, CHARLIE BROWN..

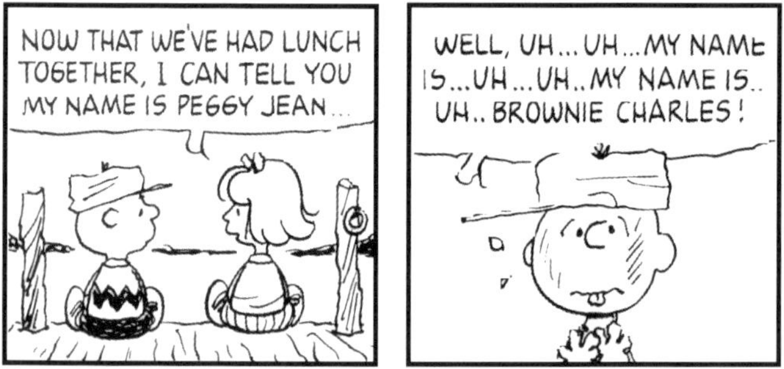
NOW THAT WE'VE HAD LUNCH TOGETHER, I CAN TELL YOU MY NAME IS PEGGY JEAN...
WELL, UH... UH... MY NAME IS... UH... UH.. MY NAME IS.. UH.. BROWNIE CHARLES!

THAT'S CUTE.. I LIKE IT..
MAYBE I'LL JUST JUMP INTO THE LAKE RIGHT HERE

AND THEN, LINUS, I GOT SO NERVOUS TRYING TO TELL HER MY NAME, I SAID IT WAS "BROWNIE CHARLES"...

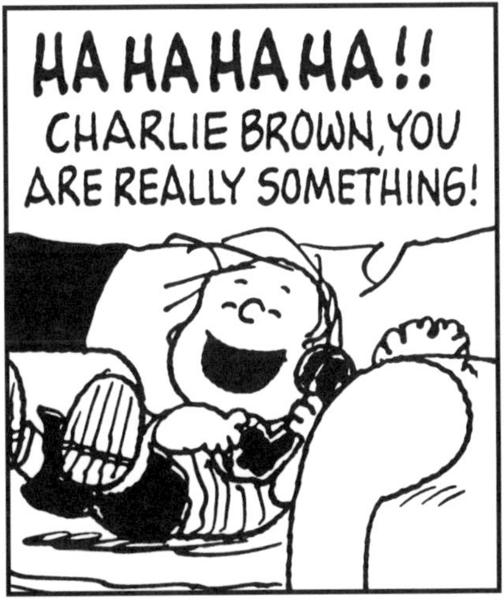
HA HA HA HA HA!!
CHARLIE BROWN, YOU ARE REALLY SOMETHING!

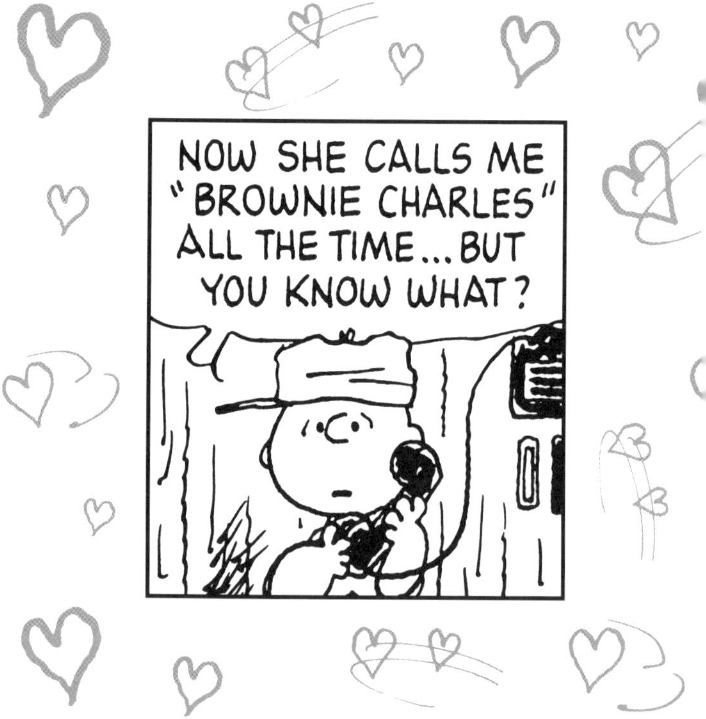
NOW SHE CALLS ME "BROWNIE CHARLES" ALL THE TIME... BUT YOU KNOW WHAT?

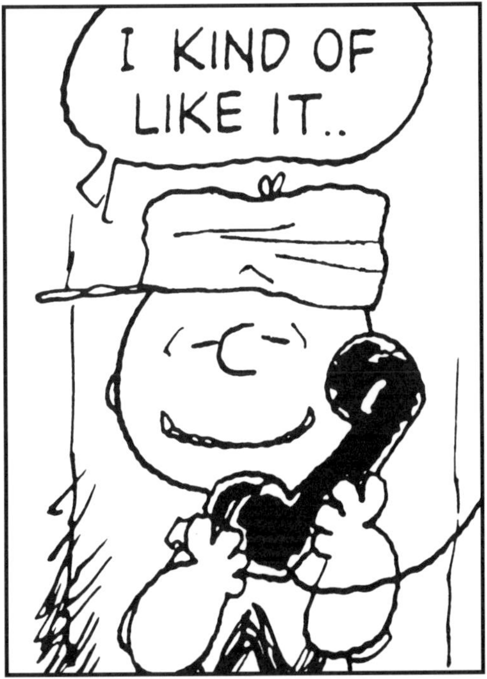
I KIND OF LIKE IT..

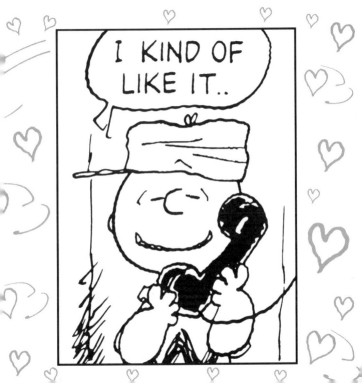

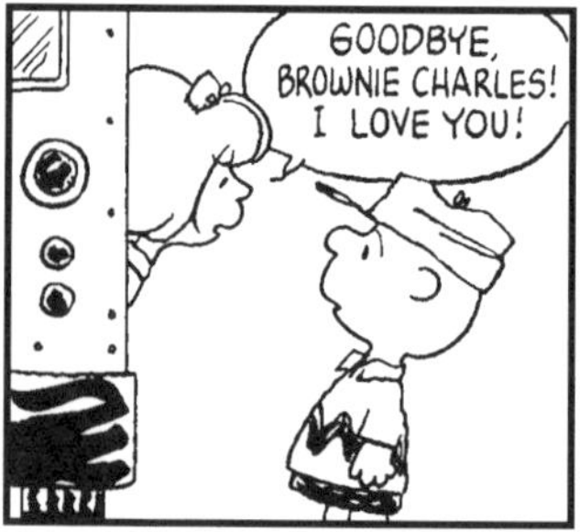
GOODBYE, BROWNIE CHARLES! I LOVE YOU!
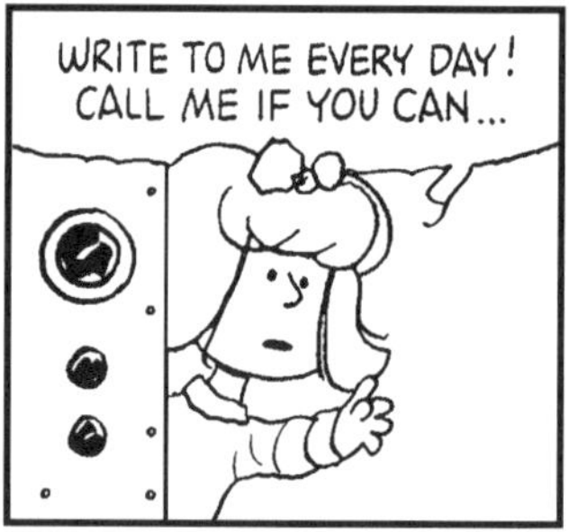
WRITE TO ME EVERY DAY! CALL ME IF YOU CAN...

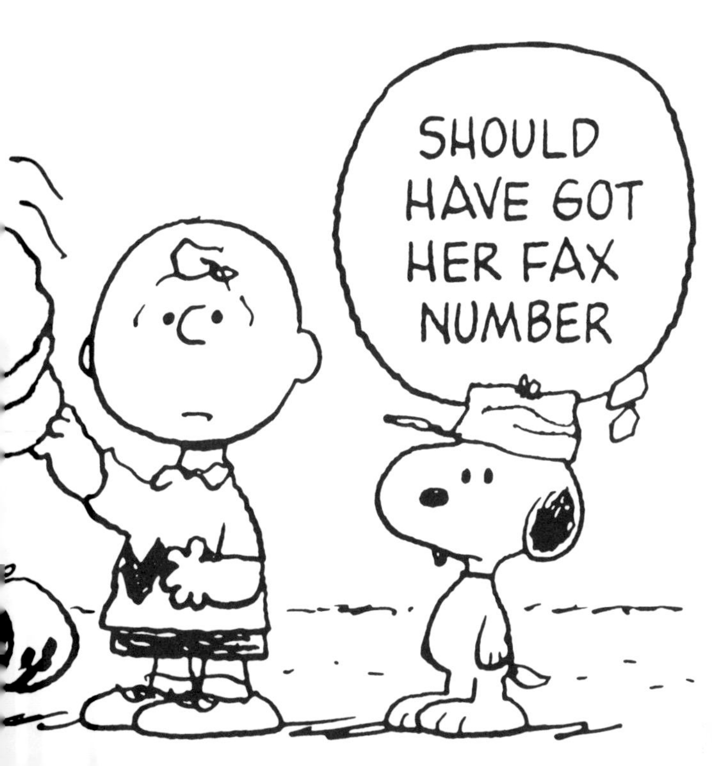
SHOULD HAVE GOT HER FAX NUMBER

First published in 1997 by HarperCollins *Publishers* Inc.  10 East 53rd Street
New York NY 10022
This edition published in 1998 by Boxtree an imprint of
Macmillan Publishers Ltd 25 Eccleston Place London SW1W 9NF and
Basingstoke

Associated companies throughout the world.

ISBN 07522 21027

3 5 7 9 8 6 4 2

A CIP catalogue record for this book is available from the British Library.

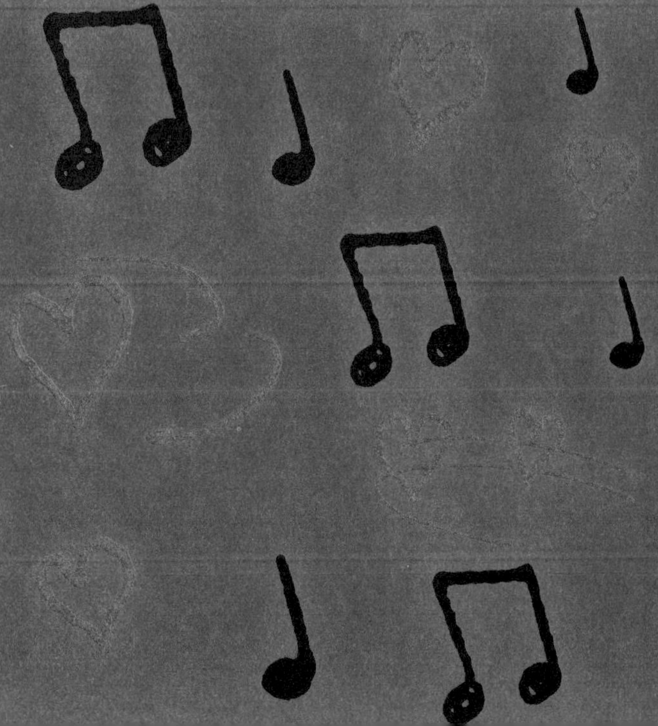

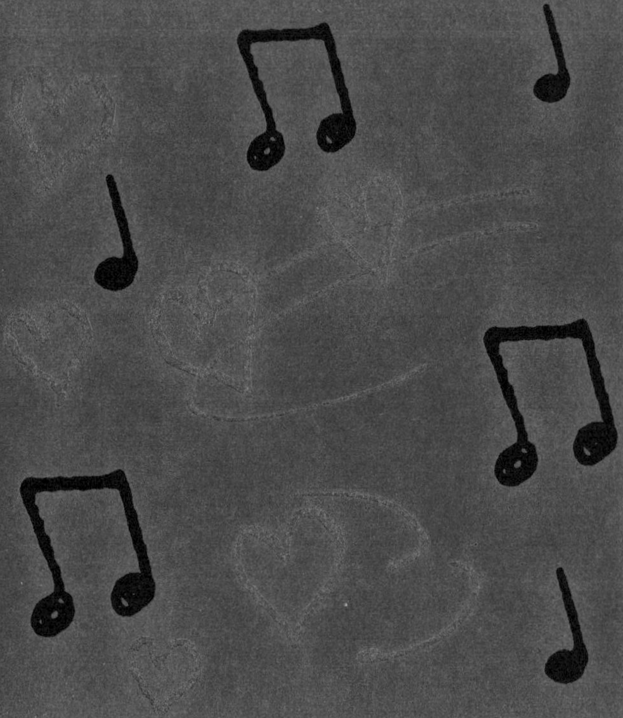